The Myth of Self-Inquiry

The Myth *of* Self-Enquiry

Questions and Answers about the Philosophy of Oneness

Jan Kersschot
Foreword by Tony Parsons

NON-DUALITY PRESS

NON-DUALITY PRESS
6 Folkestone Road Salisbury SP2 8JP United Kingdom

www.non-dualitybooks.com

Copyright © Jan Kersschot 2007
Copyright © Non-Duality Press 2007
First printing July 2007

Cover design and layout: John Gustard and Julian Noyce

For more information visit:
www.kersschot.com

Isbn 10: 0-9553999-6-3
Isbn 13: 978-0-9553999-6-1

Contents

Foreword

The Sanskrit word *"Advaita"* points to that which cannot be spoken of and exposes the fallacy of the idea that there is something separate from something else called Oneness. The simplicity of this message is directly threatening to the apparent seeker. It is rejected by the guru mind which searches for states to lay claim to ... Stillness, silence, bliss or awareness arise within the hypnotic dream of separation and then drop away again like sand through the fingers.

But Being is the one and only constant that never comes and never goes away. Because it is nothing and everything it cannot be gained or lost, given or received, approached or avoided.

The seeing of these words, the hearing of sounds, sensations in the body, feelings, thoughts ... the very stuff of boundless aliveness, is the essence of Being ... indefinable, unknowable, beyond description and yet filling every part of existence.

This clear and simple message speaks of a revolutionary perception where all traditional ideas, and even contemporary teachings of becoming something better or different, collapse. Its illumination is in the energetic, vibrant aliveness that is implicit in the wonder and liberation of simply Being.

Jan Kersschot has a clear understanding of this perception and demonstrates his ideas very well in his new book, *The Myth of Self-Enquiry*.

All the time the seeker continues to search for the unfindable through process and path this kind of exposure can be a reminder of another possibility.

Tony Parsons
April 2007

Introduction

As a child, you are told to be a person. As a reader of this book, you are told to be a person holding this book in your hands. Maybe you also imagine that you are a seeker on a spiritual path. Your spiritual leaders probably also told you that something is wrong with you. Maybe you still believe that. That you have to follow their rules in order to reach heaven. That you have to do your best in order to become worthy. That you have to meet certain standards if you want to end your spiritual search. Maybe you still believe all that as well.

Meanwhile, perhaps you have started to ask yourself questions about all the stories you once took for real. Is it all true what you've been told? Maybe you've already discovered that something was wrong with all these stories. What if time is a mind construct? What if the person is just another thought? If both the linear time axis as well as the belief in the separate person are concepts, what is left of your spiritual goals? What if there is no spiritual path at all? What if there is no path to liberation? What if the person who feels locked up is just a construction of the mind? What if spiritual liberation is just a myth?

If you believe you are in a prison, and ask me how to escape from that prison, what can I say when it's clear that the walls of that prison are made of thin air? What if all these walls were imaginary in the first place? You complain that you have a rope around your neck and that this particular rope is preventing you from becoming free. And you ask me how to remove that rope. Or you hope that I can cut that rope around your neck. What can I say when it's clear that your rope is only an imaginary rope? Do you expect me to give you a technique to untie the rope around your neck if that rope is illusory? Do you expect me to show you a path to solve your spiritual problems if that path is illusory? Can I promise you a better future as the future is an illusion? Can you expect me to approach you as a person when it's clear that that person is an illusion? Both "you" as well as the rope around your neck are illusory.

This reminds me of the story of Tashi. He is a young Buddhist monk in Ladakh, North India. The story is about the journey he made with his friend Sonam and their master Apo. In 1985, they joined the inauguration of the Shanti Stupa in Leh. The Shanti Stupa was inaugurated by the Dalai Lama that year and that's why these three monks joined the festivities. After the ceremony they stayed for a few more days and then took their horses to go back to their own monastery, Hemis Gompa, about 80 miles west of Leh. On their way home there was a big storm. They had to stop and wait until the storm was over. While they were sitting by the side of the road and waiting till the storm was over, Tashi asked his master, "How come I still have all these problems with my ego wanting to do things which are not allowed according to the rules of our monastery? What can I do to suppress them? I want to become a good monk. A devoted monk. I want to be free. I meditate as much as I can. I do the ceremonies every day – but things only get worse. Can you help me in my struggle against my ego?" The master replied, "Wait until tomorrow. Then the answer will come to you."

As the storm continued, they decided to stay over for the night. So they improvised a place to sleep in a cave and made a fire. Unfortunately, they only had two cords to tie the horses down for the night. The rope of the master's horse was gone. Probably that rope was lost during the storm. Tashi and Sonam asked their superior what to do. Apo said, "These horses are tired. I don't believe my horse will run away in the middle of the night." But the two young monks were afraid they would wake up the next morning with two horses by the tree instead of three. So Tashi and Sonam still asked their master what to do. Then Apo said, "Simply *pretend* to tie the third horse down. Pretend to take an imaginary rope from my bag and my horse will believe it's his rope you're taking. Then act as if to put it around his neck." Sonam couldn't believe what he had just heard and replied, "We just *pretend* to tie him down?" "Right. You pretend to put that *imaginary* rope around his neck and fix it to the same tree as the other two horses. Make the usual movements with your hands. Just act as if he is tied down, and my horse will stay put for the night, trust me! Although my horse is very smart, I am sure he will not move until I whistle tomorrow morning." Tashi said to Sonam, "I will do it." So Tashi pretended to tie down the third horse with an illusory rope, making the same movements as usual – as if there was a real rope involved.

Tashi and Sonam didn't sleep well that night. Not because of the storm, but because they were worrying about the master's horse. The next morning, Tashi and Sonam woke up very early and rushed to the tree. They saw that the three horses hadn't moved during the night. They were relieved to notice that they were still standing next to the tree. So the master was right when he said that the three horses wouldn't move until he whistled to them the next morning. So everything was all right. They untied their horses and they started to pack their things to continue their journey to Hemis Gompa. When the master whistled – as usual – to call the three horses, only two horses showed up. To their amazement the one horse they *pretended* to have tied down the night before did not move at all. The other two just walked towards them but the third one didn't respond to the whistle.

The two young monks were very surprised and asked, "Master, why is your horse not following the two other horses?" The master smiled and said, "That's because he still *believes* he is bound by that imaginary rope. In other words, he doesn't realize he is *not* bound." The two young monks still didn't understand. The master said, "You see, the third horse *believed* he was bound yesterday evening. You did the job very well. He didn't know that he was free to go for a walk all night long. This morning, you only untied the two horses with the real ropes, didn't you?" Tashi responded, "Yes, that's right, master – we only untied our own horses." Apo continued, "Because of the gestures you made when you pretended to tie him yesterday, the horse *still believes* himself to be bound by that imaginary rope until this very moment. He is still influenced by your hypnosis. That's why he didn't respond to my whistle." The two young monks then asked, "What should we do then?" The master responded, "Well, you just *pretend* to untie him!" Tashi laughed, but as the master insisted, he walked up to the horse and pretended to untie him. He made all the gestures with his hands as if he was really untying him. Just to make the horse *believe* he was really free now. Now the master whistled again, and his horse followed him immediately. After this, they continued their ride to the monastery.

Half an hour later, Tashi asked his master, "Do you remember that I asked you a question yesterday about my struggle against my ego? That I feel imprisoned by my fears? That I have difficulty in controlling the desires in my body? I want to find freedom in *this* life. I feel locked up in my body with its pain and its desires. I want to find my Buddha nature. I want to be free. I still didn't get an answer from you." The master replied, "Yes, I remember your question very well. The horse has given you the answer. You are like my horse." Tashi looked in amazement. Apo continued: "You see, my horse believed himself to be bound yesterday. And he believed that all night long – while he never realised that he was free all the time. That's exactly the same situation as when you ask me how to become free while you were never bound in the first place." The young monk said, "I was free all night, but I believed I was in prison? That's why you waited to give me an answer before the morning?" The master replied, "Right, Tashi. You are already free, but you just *believe* that you are bound by an illusory ego. You're bound by an illusory rope. And you complain about all the problems you believe you have with that ego. I tell you that you are free, and you don't listen. Just like my horse, you don't respond to my whistle. You believe you live in a body. You pretend to believe you are in a prison. But the walls of your prison are illusory. What you really are *is* already free. That's all you have to understand. And what can I do with monks like you? All I can do is to pretend to untie the illusory ropes around your neck until finally you respond to my whistle!"

Then there was silence for several hours. The weather was much better now, and both Tashi and Sonam looked forward to getting back home. But Sonam noticed that Tashi didn't have a smile on his face. Tashi didn't like the answer of his master. He said to his friend Sonam, "How can I already be free if I still feel bound?" Just before they reached the temple, Tashi asked his master, "What can I do to understand that I am already free?" Apo smiled. "You believe you are bound by your ego, while there *is* no ego. The ego is illusory, so you don't have to fight it or try and destroy it. The thinker you believe you are is just a thought. Your prison is empty! Don't you see? You're not imprisoned, never were, never will be, because there is no 'you' in the first place." Tashi replied, "So there is nothing I can do because there is no 'me' to do it?" Apo replied, "Exactly! If there is no Tashi, what can I say to that ghost to do to find liberation for Tashi?" Apo smiled and continued, "Just as we come back home to our temple, you come home to your true nature. And you see that you've never left home anyway."

Jan Kersschot

1 |
Are you locked up in that body?

*Q**uestioner:** Everybody says that we are an individual locked up in a body.*

Jan Kersschot: What if the sense of being locked up in a body is no more than a snapshot in your brain?

Still I feel locked up in my body.

What if the idea of being locked up in a body is no more than a few electrical currents in your brain?

Still I identify myself with my body.

The sense of being locked up in a body is very strong of course.

For example, when I look in the mirror, I see myself.

No. You only see an image of yourself. A mirror image of the front side of your body. At a few metres away from you. Is that what you really are?

When I have pain in my toe, that proves that I am in this body, doesn't it?

It only shows that at that moment there is an image of pain appearing in awareness. And that image only lasts for a moment, say less than a second. It's a snapshot. It doesn't prove anything.

But I know who I am. I am a man who is 62 years old. I have a name, I have characteristics.

Again, images in your mind. Electrical currents in your brain.

But I know I am in this body. That's what everybody told me. And it feels that way.

When you look at what appears in your story, you may notice that your body only comes to the surface during a part of the day. Your mind – your memory – says the body is there all the time, I know. But that's just another concept. Sometimes you are aware of your body. Usually because there is pain or joy.

But it's just a part of my body appearing?

When you have pain in your toe, there is an image of your toe. Not of your thyroid gland or your stomach. But when you're hungry, the stomach area appears.

I see. Only parts of my body come to my mind. Only parts of my person appear now and then.

"Your" body is not in the picture *all the time.* They're just snapshots.

But it looks as if it is continuously there.

As I said before, that's a trick of our memory.

I am not sure about that.

The body and the person appear as snapshots, as images. And then another image comes in which says that the body and mind are there *all the time.*

They come and go in our attention. They appear in awareness.

2

The story of your soul

If I am not my body, then I am a soul that has chosen this body to live in?

That's another belief. Have you ever checked? Did you ever *see* a soul? Did you ever see *your* soul? And even if you believe you have seen a soul, isn't that again another image in your mind?

All right. But I've read that my soul is going through a series of lessons.

It's another belief. Not everybody believes that. Maybe it's just a story you liked to believe.

It's true that I can't check such a story.

It's a matter of belief and hearsay. In my books, I never ask anyone to believe what I say.

For you, all these stories don't mean that much any more.

There are so many uncontrolled stories around. In a subtle way, all these stories are still about the captain. It's about *your* path. It's about *your* soul. So the ego game can go on. You want spiritual liberation. It's still about *you*. The diversity of stories that promote individualism is endless.

And anyone who dares to question all this will be labeled as a betrayer, or as someone who lost his mind. Or someone who lost faith and will go to hell.

Seekers want to continue seeking, they can't help it. And spiritual leaders just love that because it keeps the spiritual game going. The devotees can continue to play the role of being a good devotee, the leaders can continue to play the role of being a good leader.

Those who don't follow the rules are the bad guys.

The gurus don't want their devotees to ask critical questions. Nobody is allowed to question the holy texts. A lot of spiritual leaders just want the seekers to follow them, they want the devotees to believe the holy books. The devotees must believe the prophets unconditionally, and must do what they say has to be done. Just as in ordinary everyday life, we receive a to-do list. And a not-to-do list. We are again told what to do and that we will be rewarded for our good behaviour. And punished if we do not follow the rules. Again we are confirmed as being individuals with free choice who ought to do their best. And that is exactly what seekers want.

5

Some seekers, however, do not follow the crowds and are crystal clear about all this. They show us how ridiculous all these religious codes really are.

Yes, indeed.

For example, some seekers sense that there is no individual choice.

Yes.

That there is no karma. No debt to pay. No heaven and no hell.

Some also realise that there is no past or future – except as concepts in our minds.

They unmask the popular belief systems.

Some also understand that there is no body-mind in the first place. They see that each teaching that reinforces the illusion that there is such a thing as an individual starts from a basic misconception. When that fundamental misconception is seen for what it is, the whole masquerade falls apart.

That's the end of all the spiritual questions?

Some seekers seem to understand that indeed there is no seeker in the first place. Then all seeking stops automatically.

You stop seeking?

No, there is no personal involvement in this. It's not something you do. There is no "you" who can stop seeking. There is no "you" who can choose or decide to stop seeking. The seeking just disappears automatically.

Because the seeker has been seen as a ghost. It's a paradox to me.

It's not attractive for the ego when the captain is turned into a ghost. When they hear about it, most readers quickly turn their backs. The reader doesn't like to be unmasked and prefers to continue to play its games.

Why do they walk away from the truth?

The ego doesn't want to die. And the individual path is much more attractive!

They want to keep seeking. Maybe that's what all these temples and ceremonies are for. To keep these people on the spiritual path.

When it is clear that there is no captain, it is obvious that there is no spiritual path either. But again, most seekers don't like the idea.

3|

The fight against
the shadow side

Once you said in a conversation that there is no black without white, no bad without good. I can accept that from a theoretical point of view. But does this mean that you are against helping other people?

No, of course not.

That's what people sometimes conclude when they hear about or read your books.

It means they haven't understood what I was trying to say. There is only one. If you help someone else, you're helping yourself. If you attack someone it's like attacking yourself.

There is only one player.

If you fight someone, it's like cutting off your own toe. I compared it to one giant octopus with 6.5 billion arms. There is only one consciousness and 6.5 billion actors. And the apparent good and bad are only labels. Life itself isn't either good or bad, it just is. It's neutral.

Still most people on this planet don't seem to understand that these negative energies are in balance with positive energies. Although it's clear to me now that there is always a balance between left and right.

Because the division between left and right is just in your mind. In my mind. In their mind.

I see.

Sooner or later, spiritual leaders come up with a plan to get rid of all these negative energies – without realizing that such a plan itself exactly confirms the sense of separation. All these games are (apparently of course) destroying the sense of Unicity and creating a path in order to restore that Oneness. While Oneness has never been divided.

I see. Now I also understand why they might not like your books.

First they create a division between left and right. Then they say that left is bad and right is good. And then they claim that they are standing on the right side!

It's crazy. The human mind plays such wonderful tricks.

And then they will come up with a plan. They will

9

show you a path or a method to create more of the right side and a method to destroy the left side. While the division between left and right is just in their heads.

I see. It's a line in their head.

Maybe they will tell you that those who are standing on the left side of the line are wrong.

When you look at it that way, it's ridiculous.

What I am trying to tell you is not complicated. No left without right. I believe that's the way it is. It's quite simple. As soon as you create the left side in your head, there is a right side.

4|

Intelligent design versus Darwinism

Your books deal with several philosophical and spiritual questions, but they don't deal with the big questions. For example, regarding the origin of the universe. How did the earth come to be? Where do we come from? Has it all been designed? These are important issues for me.

As far as I know, intelligent design is a belief system proposed mainly by Christian apologists who feel science and more particularly Darwin's evolution theory threatens their Biblical-based view of the world.

I'm surprised by how much publicity the intelligent design movement has received in the last 10 years, especially in America.

They must have a very good public relations machine.

There are some people in Seattle at the Discovery Institute with an annual publicity budget of a few million dollars aimed at persuading Newsweek *and* Time *magazine that the whole scientific community is talking about intelligent design. These people want to exclude evolution from the public school curriculum and put "creation science" in its place to convince young students that the Bible has been proven exactly right.*

It's amazing that this is happening in the 21st century. If I am right, these creationists believe that our universe is just six thousand years old, every species was fashioned by God in seven days, and a worldwide flood later drowned all creatures except one mating pair of each kind. I find that hard to believe.

In an earlier conversation, you said to me that from your early childhood on you were looking for an absolute wisdom, not a limited wisdom. You said that you didn't want to accept a wisdom that is only true for one group of people.

Right. Those who believe the Bible is the word of God may use all sorts of arguments to prove they're right. But what about the Hindus? They have their Vedas which are said to be much older than the Bible. They have their own story of how the world was created. So I believe it's a waste of energy to discuss whether the proponents of "intelligent design" are right or not.

If you don't believe in intelligent design, do you prefer to believe in Darwinism and the big bang?

It all depends on whether you believe in time or whether you really see that the concept of a linear time axis is a construction of the human mind.

How do you mean?

Both the religious point of view as well as the scientific theory are based on a linear time axis. Without a concept of the past, they mean nothing! You know that in my books time is exposed as a mind construct. Even when you think about yesterday, that particular thought is appearing *presently*. Even if you reflect on what happened two minutes ago, such thoughts appear *in the moment*. Not in the past. Nobody ever lived in the past. You can *think* about the past, but such a thought doesn't appear in the past. You may think about the big bang or imagine a holy being creating this universe, but these thoughts are still images *appearing now* and not thousands or billions of years ago.

That sounds a bit easy, doesn't it? There are important discussions going on these days - especially in the US - regarding intelligent design versus Darwinism. You can't just throw both away like that. Suppose we accept the existence of time for theoretical reasons.

OK. Still it is allowable to ask critical questions about what others believe in, isn't it?

Those who believe in intelligent design say that there must be a God behind it all. And some of them also say that it is all described in the Bible.

Isn't it difficult to believe that Eve was created from Adam's rib?

Well, yes.

I can understand that people believed this in the middle ages. But today, in the Western world?

Science has proved religion wrong a long time ago, hasn't it?

If people are willing to believe in Adam and Eve now, they are willing to believe *anything* they're told. Anatomically, men and women have the same number of ribs – twenty-four. When this fact was noted by the Flemish anatomist Vesalius in the 16th century, it sparked off a wave of controversy, as it seemed to contradict Genesis.

You mean that those who still believe in this story now lack scientific education?

Well, they are willing to accept a lot of stories without any discrimination at all. The story of Noah's ark when the whole planet was flooded, for example.

I can't imagine that the Himalayas were flooded. The story says that when Noah was six hundred years old, God decided to send a great flood to destroy all life. God was angered at the wickedness of mankind. But God told Noah to build a vessel for himself and his family, and for two of every sort of animal. It's even more ridiculous than the story of Adam and Eve.

If Adam and Eve were both white, where do all these

black and yellow people come from? There are so many stories around.

Each religion has its own story about the creation of the world. The Jews say it happened 5,767 years ago, the Hindus have a completely different story. The Hindus say we are now in the fourth and last cycle, the Kali Yuga, which is 432,000 years long.

Which one is true? If all these religions present us with so many different hypotheses, I prefer to believe the scientists. At least, they try to be critical.

So you believe in the big bang theory?

Well, yes and no. I would only accept that as a theory if we accept the existence of time.

It's another theory?

If scientists say it all started with a big bang billions of years ago, I would like to ask them what was there *before* the big bang? And what exactly did explode?

I see.

Even when scientists today come up with the "string theory" containing 11 dimensions, that's still a theory in the mind of those scientists.

Right. They're just inventing new theories within existing theories. New games within the existing games.

15

It's endless. They can go on and on and find even more new theories and mathematical models to describe the cosmos. Each time more sophisticated than the previous theory, each time a bit closer to the truth. But whatever they observe or discover or describe, all of it appears on the same white screen as everything else.

They don't seem to realise that.

All of it is appearing on the same plasma screen like everything else. But these scientists never ask themselves any questions about the screen.

Anyway, such a search is endless. You can always dig deeper.

It's like trying to find the edge of our universe. It's a never-ending story.

OK. I see what you mean.

The major point here is our belief in a linear time axis. No thought ever appeared 5 seconds ago. No scientific experiment ever happened in the past.

It's always happening now!

Past and future are in our minds, not "out there" in the world. So what is the value of the scientific theory about the origin of the universe – no matter how sophisticated their tools or how complicated their hypothesis

– if we really understand the full consequences of the fact that the past is a mind construct?

On the other hand, there appears to be an intelligent design in nature, doesn't there?

Yes, absolutely! There *appears* to be an intelligent design.

It's a wonderful creation, isn't it?

Right. That's why people project a director behind this creation. An engineer who developed all this. They say that if there is a movie, there must be a director. A creator. And if you look at the world, it's amazing.

That's maybe why the creationists are popular.

There appears to be an intelligent design in nature and everything, but why not leave it like that? Everything *is*. Stay with that childlike wonderment. Then creation *is* a wonder. It *is* a wonder to see how complicated everything is – the structure of DNA, the fact that we can see, that we can breathe, the oceans and mountains, all these creatures on this planet, the stars and milky ways. I agree it's a wonder. Simply the fact that things appear is wonderful. We take it for granted, but the fact that there *is* an appearance is a wonder. It's stunning. Everything is magic when you realize that. Maybe my words sound childish to you but I don't need any holy books to recognize the wonder of life. The wonder of mere existence. It is amazing that things and people *are*. That's what is holy to me: to be. *Beingness.* Just *to be*. Do you need a holy book and a messiah for that childlike wonderment? Why do we need a designer who was there before creation?

So you don't believe in Darwin and you don't believe in a divine creation?

Both are consolation prizes for those who still believe in a linear time axis. Past and future are in our heads. Time is very practical for the organization of everyday life, but the concepts of past and future are not interesting when we're talking about nondualism. When you ask me about the nature of Oneness, these concepts become obstacles. Once it is clear there is only Oneness, all these theories become obsolete. I know it sounds easy but it *is* easy – there is only "this." And *this* means just what appears in awareness. It's the current image on the plasma screen. All there is, is that which appears. The rest is based on theories, habits and beliefs.

So the story about a God having created everything is not true? That's what the Bible says.

You rely on the books, not on what "you" see. The experiments in *"Coming Home"* invite you to see for yourself instead of believing what others have said. It's up to you to check it out. It's like a scientific experiment. You can repeat the experiments as often as you like. And once there is "seeing" you don't need my books any more. Then it's all obvious.

Still the idea of a higher being creating and guiding every-thing has always been very popular.

Who created this creator then? At some point, people will get stuck when you ask critical questions. Where does this creator come from? How come there are so many different gods around? And suppose that there might have been a creator creating the universe – then that creator would be separate from its creation. Where is the border between the two?

You don't see any border between "what is" on the one hand and God on the other? No demarcation line between creation and the creator? Is that what you're trying to tell me?

Have you seen the line? You can try to see the border and then come back and tell me. Can you show me that line?

No.

Do you see the demarcation line on the movie screen?

No.

The white screen in front of the movie theatre hasn't any lines on it.

The white screen doesn't cut the images into two sides.

In the metaphor of the movie screen, the white screen stands for pure awareness. And the light in the back of the theatre for the creator.

So I could say then that god is the light at the back of the movie theatre and that "your" movie is appearing on the white screen. For me, that was a first step in my understanding.

But you know that I don't want to describe it as steps, because then it sounds like a process.

I know.

So you believed that god was the light at the back of the movie theatre and that your movie was appearing on the white screen in the front.

But I was still projecting myself as a viewer in the theatre. I mean, I still thought of myself as someone sitting on a seat. In between the two, so to speak.

That's a popular view.

After doing the experiments in your book, I saw myself as a witness of my movie. A lot of other seekers I talked with also believed that they were "looking at the world" instead of being involved. It felt a bit "cold."

You were still identifying with the witness.

There was still a duality between me and the images.

Right.

There was also a duality between me and the creator. I saw my awareness as the witness, the images in front of me and the lamp of light behind me.

Two demarcation lines. One between you and the images in front of you and another line between you and the lamp of light in the back. Once again, images in the mind.

Yes! My life in front of me and God behind me. I was still identifying with my "me" sitting in between.

I see.

After all, it was not that bad. At least that vision made it clear to me that there is only one light shining on all these billions of movies. I already "saw" that there was only one light source for all human beings. Not a different lamp for each religion. But now I see there were other insights still to come. One evening, a few months ago, you said to me that this image of "myself" was again another projection of the mind.

You were surprised, although it's obvious once it's seen.

You also said that the person I believed I was is not sitting on a chair somewhere between the screen and the lamp. You said that my personality was just one of the ten thousand images on the screen.

You didn't like me saying that, did you?

No, I didn't like it at all. You reduced me to some coloured spots on a white screen.

The ego doesn't like to be pointed at as an image. As a snapshot.

I thought of myself as someone important. To see that you're no more than a snapshot on a screen is not an easy one.

The personality is indeed nothing more than an image. A concept.

Now it's obvious to me. Well, I shouldn't say "to me" of course. Anyway, the person sitting on his chair between his movie and the lamp was a ghost.

As I've said before, the metaphor of the movie screen and the lamp is only a metaphor. The light and the images on the movie screen are not separate. They're like a plasma screen.

That's the "real" philosophy of Oneness for me.

It's too simple to deserve the description "philosophy." It was a journalist in Holland who used the term when he wrote an article about my book in a Dutch journal on yoga.

I can't understand why it took me so long to see something so obvious.

There are no borders, there is only Unicity. Does that sound difficult?

There are no demarcation lines. Never were, never will be.

There are no demarcation lines, except in our minds.

So, no demarcation line between creation and creator, right?

Both creation and the creator appear in the same Oneness because Oneness is all-encompassing. If Oneness is all-encompassing there can't be anything outside of it.

What about God then?

Well, I would say that there are two possibilities. One: both the creator and creation appear as concepts in the same Oneness. Then, God is just a concept in your mind. One of the ten thousand images that day. Two: God equals Oneness.

I prefer the latter, because then God is everything.

And it's obvious that there is only one God then.

5 |

Blasphemy

*I accept there is only one God. One God who created
everything. You said that this one single God knows no
borders, and must be infinite. I accept that as well. So this
God is the same as your sense of beingness.*

Well, it's not a *sense* of beingness I refer to, it is Beingness with a capital I refer to. It's That in which everything appears. It is everything.

So God is the same as Beingness.

Right. But I prefer the word Beingness because it
sounds more neutral than Brahman or God.

*But then I also have to accept that I am that single infinite
God, because you said that Oneness equals Beingness and
in your books I've discovered that I am this very Beingness.*

What you really are is that Beingness, yes.

Blasphemy

If I tell that to my priest, he would say that I believe I am God! Isn't that blasphemy then?

No. Blasphemy means that you *as a person* believe you're God. This is just the opposite.

How do you mean? You said in your book "This Is It" that you are Beingness. And that Beingness equals God. So I conclude that you believe yourself to be God.

You're mixing up things. I am not talking about "me" – as the character Jan – identifying with Beingness. That would be ridiculous. It's the "real me" that is Oneness. It's not you as a person who will reach this. That's exactly the core of this philosophy of Oneness.

I don't understand.

You have to disappear first – so to speak – before the understanding appears that you are Beingness. I know it sounds like a paradox. That's why this "philosophy of oneness" doesn't deserve the description "philosophy." It's full of inconsistencies.

Still some people will say that what you say is blasphemous.

The word blasphemy means, for example, claiming the attributes of a deity, or showing contempt or lack of reverence for God.

You mean, it's insulting the spiritual leaders or their gods.

25

Yes.

Aren't you doing that?

No, not at all. When it's clear that everything is as it should be, why would I want to fight or insult the gods or the churches?

Still, I felt attacked by your books.

What I write about in my books may take away your faith in spiritual dogmas because I invite you to have a look for yourself. But I am not trying to ridicule the religions or their leaders or their books. I say that everybody is free to believe what they want to believe in. I also say that I am not trying to change that. If that wasn't clear, I want to say it once again.

It's OK. I see what you mean. I have it now.

But what I do in my books is pointing at what you can see for yourself. It's like a scientific experiment. I invite you to have a look. Without any prejudices. One of the experiments invites you to see if there is a person living in your body.

I remember. It's called "nobody home."

One of the conclusions in that chapter is that there is no separate person. So how could Jan ever claim to be God, when two minutes earlier I said that this Jan is just an image on the screen?

So it's not blasphemy at all?

It's not you *as a person* who discovers she is God. It's you *as you really are* that equals Beingness. It's *what you really are* which is God. And that God is not you as a person but equals the one Beingness I was referring to before. But not God as an idea, not Beingness as a concept in your mind, but Oneness without borders. The unthinkable One.

But the belief of a higher being creating and guiding everything has always been very popular. I liked the idea, really.

Why make it an outside agency? Where is this God then? And again, where are the borders?

I don't know. Nobody ever asked me such questions.

Where does God come from then?

Well, they say that...

Can you give an answer to these questions without relying on religious dogmas or holy books?

The designer could have created himself?

Created out of what? Out of nothing? Do you really believe all that?

That's what they say. Out of nothingness. It's true that it is impossible. It sounds nice but it's silly.

Sooner or later you may discover that a lot of these beliefs are stories based on belief and hearsay. If you examine them carefully, there isn't much left of them.

How can people still believe all that in the 21st century? Some of them even want to die for that belief.

If you look at all the stories and rules and holy books with a critical mind, can you still continue to believe in all these stories about heaven and hell?

Each religion has its own rules and customs, and their own infallible creator. But it's hard to convince these people that their belief is just a mind construct.

Yes indeed.

Even when these believers see that they have no solid proof, they still go on with their holy book in their hands. They strongly hold on to their dogmas.

It's not a problem we have to solve. We are not better than they are. We don't have to try and change them.

I see.

Everybody can make his own image of a creator in his mind and give him the name he prefers.

And some believers are very serious about that. They wouldn't appreciate what you just said.

They can't help it if they want to hold onto their belief systems.

That's how they are programmed.

And that's OK. That's how it is.

That's how they're designed.

They can't help it either that they appear as they appear.

Let it be.

I am not inviting you to disrespect them.

6 |

What to do after the understanding

I liked your books, but I was disappointed that in the end of the book you didn't give me any suggestion as to how to live my life. Why didn't you do that? It would have been a much better book if you had done so.

It's just the opposite. Apparently you haven't understood anything of what I was trying to say in those books. If I were to tell you what to do, the whole book would become ridiculous. Saying there is only Oneness, that there are no hierarchies, and then telling people how to behave. Don't you see it is ridiculous? When it is clear that there is only Oneness, there can't be any rules to be followed.

It's not that easy to let go of all these precious stories and religious traditions. I don't want to throw away all these ceremonies and all this culture that is related to my religion.

You don't have to throw away anything. You can pretend to believe whatever you like. You believe you have to pray five times a day. That's OK. You prefer to believe you are a sinner? That's OK. You believe you will go to hell if you don't follow the rules? That's OK.

You talk about this as if all religions are inventions. That these holy books have no reality. That all these followers of these religions are fools. You should respect them.

I don't write books about what others believe in. There are thousands of books like that. I try to write about nondualism. About that which can't be cut into two pieces.

You should respect the religions and their followers for who they are.

I do. They're free to believe in whatever they want to believe. I am not trying to convince them to leave their church or temple.

But you also suggest that religions don't help people find the ultimate truth.

I believe they're pointing to themselves. To keep their own system running.

Do you feel superior because you can unmask their systems in your books?

No, not at all. I've said before that one of the insights I write about is the seeing that we are all equal. How could I feel superior?

OK.

Don't think that my words are better than what others have told you. It doesn't matter what you believe or see. Oneness doesn't care if you see there is only Oneness or not.

Oneness doesn't care?

This impersonal boundless Energy is everywhere. Right here, right now, is Oneness appearing. No matter if your apparent person likes its world or not. No matter what your holy book says. What is happening presently *is It*. There is nothing other! It's so simple and obvious. Nothing is lacking, nobody is unworthy – despite the appearances.

You said, "Nobody is unworthy." Does that also mean that after the understanding there are no more sins on the spiritual level?

No more guilt, no more striving, no more sins. You still have to stop your car for a red light – practical matters don't change – but you can forget about karma, heaven and hell.

I find that hard to believe.

That's OK. You may try and engineer your spiritual path, try to follow the rules of your religious tradition, but that too will still be "what is." All of it is just another image in the apparent story, immediately replaced by the next image.

It's all a dream then. That's what they sometimes say. Are we just dreaming during the day, just as we believe in dream characters in the night? Are we watching an opera? Is it all a daydream?

I use the metaphor of life as a movie a lot because for some people it makes things clear.

Is the movie just a story we create in our minds?

If some say that everything is created in the mind, that all is an illusion, they usually forget to add that their self-image is also an illusion. The one who says that everything is an illusion, is itself also an illusion. The thinker in your head is a ghost.

The ego is also an image on the screen?

Exactly. That's how *unimportant* you are as a person.

I see.

When that is clear, can I still say you have to meditate for twenty minutes twice a day?

If the person is only a mirage appearing on the screen for a few milliseconds, it's not some entity that will go to hell or to heaven. Is that what you're trying to say?

What you truly are is boundless – despite the appearances. It's not limited to your character.

And this boundlessness doesn't need to go anywhere?

Where can the infinite go when it is already every-where?

OK, but I want to get closer to Beingness. What should I do?

How can you come closer to what you are?

Well, I don't know.

How can I tell you what to do in order to express this Beingness if it is clear that it is already happening?

Do we have to stop taking spiritual things seriously then?

You don't have to stop anything. Even when you don't take the opera seriously, still the show goes on. The apparent Jan still has apparent problems or apparent desires. In the movie. In the appearance.

It's no more than a movie?

But life continues to *look* real, even when you see it is a movie.

Pain is still painful, joy is still joyful, and so on.

Pain still appears as pain, joy still appears as joy. The story seems to continue, with laughter and blood, with tears and music and everything. But it is clear that whatever happens in the movie does not happen to the actor – it is just a series of images on a screen.

The pain is not real then?

Pain still appears as pain, but it's not *your* pain. There is pain appearing as an image on the screen. Joy still appears as joy, but it's not *your* joy. There is just an image of joy appearing. It is just another image on the screen.

And I feel it's my pain?

That's just the next image, coming after the pain and saying, "This is my pain." That's the inner voice. I sometimes describe it as the subtitles in your movie.

They're just subtitles. They don't mean anything.

In some cases, the subtitles are "expanding" in such a way that they fill the whole image.

In that case, people only notice their own comments. They don't see what they see or don't feel what they feel because they are hypnotized by what their inner voice is saying. They're overwhelmed by their own comments.

Anyway, pain still appears as pain; it is still painful and "your" body may not like it because it is programmed that way. But it's not *your* pain.

I don't like you saying that to me.

The same goes for joy. Joy still appears as joy – it is still joyful and "your" body may like it because it is programmed that way. But it's not *your* joy.

I am not involved any more!

The story simply happens on the screen and the apparent ego is just another snapshot. The story is made of Light, and as such it is what I really am: boundless Energy, endless Light, unbroken Unicity.

What about my personal past then?

The movie is supposed to look real. Sensations of your body and personal feelings are tools to make it look real. Space and time are another set of tools to make it look real. The mind makes us believe that the past has happened before, but that story is itself an image appearing *now* - with the subtitle "in the past." Have you ever lived in the past? Your memory is playing a game with you and you don't realize it is doing so! It's a trick of the mind. Memory makes us believe that there is a linear time axis. But there isn't! It's just an idea. The belief you're locked up in a body is also a concept. It's also an idea, an image passing by in "your" movie.

They're all uncontrolled ideas?

Your bodily sensations, thoughts, emotions – they're all images appearing on that same plasma screen.

7 |

Can a ghost
become enlightened?

You keep on saying again and again that there is no individuality, except in the appearance. I don't see the point of that.

There is no point to it.

Really? I find that hard to accept. I want something to do.

There is no goal. Everything just is. Everything *is*.

You take away my ambitions. All my personal insights.

There is no personal path. No plan.

If that were true, there would be nothing left to do on the spiritual level. All these religious dogmas lose their meaning. Everything is possible then.

That's exactly why some call it liberation.

That's what I want: liberation.

But not liberation for the individual. Because the individual is an illusion.

Right. Just liberation.

As there is more clarity about the illusory aspect of the individual, there is less fractionating and dividing of life. As a result, there are less attempts to engineer our life story on a spiritual level. Before wc see that the individual has no absolute value, we approach spirituality as businessmen. We always expect a return. We want to know more, we want to make changes for the better, get something for ourselves, work for a better world, reach a higher level of awareness for ourselves or for the human population, fight against evil and so on. After seeing that there is only Oneness, everything is allowed to be as it is. The deal is over. Life can flow freely now. There is still the appearance of a personal story, but it's clear that it's only an appearance.

So life just happens then.

The endless fight against "life as it is" is over. Apparent deeds are still done, apparent thoughts are still arising, apparent problems are still appearing on the movie screen, but on the spiritual level there is no business plan any more.

What is the effect on the seeker?

That the idea of being on a spiritual path is just a concept of the mind. An illusion. Not only the spiritual path is illusory, also the seeker is an illusion. In other words, it's the complete end of the spiritual search.

To me, it sounds unbelievable. But for those who are not spiritual seekers, what you are saying wouldn't mean much to them.

That's why this understanding is not a big deal for those who are not on a spiritual path.

Why is there all that spiritual seeking then?

Since the day you accepted from your parents and teachers and bathroom mirrors that you were limited to your body and mind, there was something lacking in life. You apparently lost your true nature. You went from boundlessness to a limited entity.

That's how our minds got programmed.

The mind is full of programmes which split Oneness into duality. The major one splits the world into "me" and "the rest of the world."

OK. When I was born, there was only oneness. And then my mind got programmed and duality appeared.

Maybe you are aware of that, maybe you're not.

Oneness isn't apparent any more to me and then I go and look for it?

There may be a sense that something fundamental is missing. And some may try to fill that emptiness inside.

We miss the original openness we had as a baby. How do we try to fill this gap?

Some people want to possess as many objects as they can. That may give them a sense that they've been successful. Others look for emotional richness.

So people look for material or emotional satisfaction to compensate for the inner emptiness or lack of fulfillment they feel.

We can't generalize. It's different for everyone. What I point to is just one of the mechanisms.

There are many ways to get rid of this sense of inner lack. Ways of giving meaning to life.

One can also give meaning to life by fulfilling a social role in the community.

It's different for everyone.

Right – in the appearance. Remember we're still talking about actors, not about "real" people.

The actor can give meaning to his or her life by getting married, and taking care of their partner and children, for example. Or taking care of their parents.

Yes. By taking care of other people. By doing some social work. Others want to become famous, or have power. Still others give meaning to their life by helping people who are in pain, by defending their country, by organizing a crusade, by doing research, by helping the poor, by building a temple, by going into politics. For some, material and psychological satisfaction is not enough. They look for a deeper meaning.

They become a monk. Or a priest.

For example. They look for a higher plan. For themselves or for the planet. Some want to join a spiritual organization. Some sense something more fundamental is lacking – whether they're conscious of that or not.

These are the ones who become spiritual seekers. And read all the books about spirituality.

Some of them start to read books about meditation. Some follow a course in yoga. Others would rather go to a temple or church. Some are willing to do what the spiritual leaders tell them to do. Or accept whatever the holy books have said.

And yet, for some, that's still not enough.

They are still not satisfied. They realise that what the leader of their church is telling them is leading them up the garden path. So they have to dig deeper.

They look for a guru.

Someone who really knows.

They need a living teacher. This is especially true in the Eastern traditions. A so-called awakened being who can answer all their questions. They want the ultimate awakening. These seekers want enlightenment. They look for the ultimate freedom.

And even then, they're still not satisfied. Most of them still sense that something is missing.

These are the seekers you wrote your books for. For those who have tried everything.

I try to make them aware of several traps. For example, that their search is still about themselves.

How do you mean?

In the search for freedom, such an "advanced" spiritual seeker is attracted to a teacher who promotes the ego.

You mean that the ego is still behind the steering wheel?

The seeker wants to be confirmed as a seeker and will be attracted to a teaching which reinforces the idea of being an individual.

The ego doesn't want to die?

Can a Ghost Become Enlightened?

The seeker is willing to follow the rules. Most seekers are willing to give up a life of luxury, the joy of sex and all the rest - except one thing: the identification with a separate identity with free will and personal choice.

Their ego is stronger than their need for fulfillment?

They still hold onto their body and soul and don't want to give up all the common beliefs that are related to *their* life. To *their* soul.

They don't want to let go of their story, their individual path?

Yes, indeed. The path is still about "me," about *my* sense of inner lack, about *my* search, *my* prayers, *my* karma.

Is it all a game then? Just another trick of the mind?

That's one way to look at this.

Human history is filled with religions and sects and belief systems. They all say the opposite of what you say.

Well, they won't tell their followers that there is no path to follow, because then they would undermine their own system. So they will tell you what to do. And what to avoid.

These are the spiritual rules. People seem to believe all these religious dogmas.

43

It's attractive for the mind. It all seems so real. The prayers, the mantras, the holy texts. That's the power of the daydream.

That's the power of mass hypnosis. A lot of grown-ups join the game and they seem to stimulate each other by confirming their egos.

The movie of life is designed that way.

We are supposed to believe we are really limited to this personality. And this continues in the spiritual search. While you say that the end of the search will bring us exactly to the understanding that this "little self" is an illusion.

But the ego has a lot of mechanisms to keep up appearances. The seeker doesn't like to hear that the seeker is a ghost. That the soul is a concept in the mind.

The ego will use all its tools to attack these ideas. To keep the sense of self alive. The ego needs dualism to stay alive.

And as long as this sense of self looks real, this message of nondualism will not penetrate.

And one keeps on searching for improvement of the ego. Or for salvation of the soul.

This holding on to the false self will automatically lead to a teaching or religion which claims that it can bring the devotee to the promised salvation. All these stories are very popular because they confirm our sense of self. The seeker wants to be confirmed continuously as being a person. A person with a past and a future.

The seeker wants to be confirmed continuously as being a seeker!

Right.

How come I didn't see this before? It's always about the seeker. It's so obvious and still nobody ever told me this. I always took the stories people told me for real.

And these stories suit the seeker well. It's food for the ego. Usually such a teaching will promise enlightenment through discipline, hard work and sacrifice. It gives the seeker hope that he or she will finally reach Oneness - in the future.

That is the game.

That's the carrot on the stick.

And most seekers believe that following the rules can lead them to the top of the mountain.

When the promised ultimate experience of enlightenment is still not reached after several decades of seeking, some seem to put a question mark beside these teachings. Others will try and find another story to explain why "it" hasn't happened yet, such as "It will happen in my next life," or "Only a few are really chosen" or "I still have a long way to go because I have a lot of personal shortcomings", or "I have to remove some more bad karma first." Any excuse that promotes further seeking will do. And all sorts of books and teachings will confirm this, of course. It's again the popular dream of personal evolution.

8

You can believe whatever
you like to believe

I am Jewish and I still hold on to my religion.

I don't mind if you do. I am not saying it's bad for
you.

*We believe that there is a single, omniscient, omnipotent,
omnibenevolent God, who created the universe and continues to be involved in its governance. He also established
a covenant with the Jewish people, and revealed his laws
and commandments to them in the form of the Torah. So
the Torah is not just another holy book, you know.*

That's what you've been told. That's what you and a
few other million people believe.

*The practice of Judaism is devoted to the study and obser-
vance of the laws and commandments in the Torah. My
religion is the first recorded monotheistic faith. Did you
know it is one of the oldest monotheistic religious traditions still practised today?*

It is also the foundation of Christianity and Islam, isn't it?

But these three religions are very different. We have our own moral codes and habits. I definitely believe if I don't live according to the rules, I will end up in hell when I die. For example, I will never mix meat with milk in one dish. And I never eat lobster or oysters.

Why is that? Is a lobster less an expression of God's creation than a chicken? Is a pig "of a lower cast" than a cow?

The laws of keeping "kosher" are the Jewish dietary laws. These involve the abstention from consuming animals that eat other animals, and that roam the sea floor eating the excretions of other animals. Also, mixing meat and milk is not allowed.

You can believe whatever you like to believe. Or hold onto what others have told you to believe.

I still believe it's important that I live according to the rules of my community. It's important for my soul. For my spiritual future.

I am not saying it's wrong to obey the rules. Maybe you're still thinking in terms of "me" and "the others."

I know. I only realise that right now.

You prefer the self-hypnosis. You – well, your apparent ego – wants to keep on daydreaming. Your mind is driven by memory, habits and hearsay. Maybe you are holding on to "your" past and "your" future. On to "your" people. Your tradition. Maybe you're still thinking in terms of "the good people" and "the bad people." All I do in my books is point to Oneness. I point to That which is "all of us," no matter if you are Hindu, Christian or Jew. This Oneness can't divide things or people. Oneness doesn't exclude anyone or anything!

Can I change my vision? I mean, I would also like to see that. I feel as if I am indeed under some kind of hypnosis. We are programmed by our religion at a very young age, you know. I want to wake up from the daydream. Maybe that's why I am talking to you now, I don't know. Can I do something to understand it as well, just like you and a few others?

It doesn't work that way. You still want "it" for yourself. You want to join the club of the "free souls." It's nothing like that at all. I don't see myself as any better than anyone else. So you are not less than someone who sees through the daydream. So, to me, you don't have to change. You can still go to your synagogue every week. You don't have to change your diet. You can continue to live according to the rules of your holy books.

What I eat, how much I pray, it's not essential? Is that what you're saying?

Not essential to Beingness. It may be important for your spiritual leaders.

49

Let me tell you something. We don't have any spiritual leaders! Our authority is not vested in any person but rather in the Torah.

Well, in that case, your priests in your local synagogue still may not like what I say to you. Whatever you do, eat or not eat, it may be part of your culture. And that's all OK. But it won't bring you closer to heaven.

I also do the ritual bath following menstruation every month.

I take a shower every day. But not to clean my soul. You see, all these rituals are endless. Why can't you take a shower during menstruation?

I don't know.

There are so many different customs, rules and habits. Each religion has its own.

But don't I need all these rules to find salvation?

I don't think so. Some can't eat pork, others can't eat cow, others can't eat lobsters, others are not allowed to drink alcohol. Do all these rules sound like the absolute truth to you? If you look for a truth or an understanding which is true for *everyone*, all these habits lose their importance.

I see.

They all have their own way of getting rid of their sins. They all have their own story about how to avoid hell and how to make sure of going to heaven.

But in our religion, we are told that we have to ...

What about all the other believers who believe they have to work on their karma or pray in another temple, also to reach salvation? Are they children of a lesser god then?

I see. I may as well give it all up.

You don't have to give up anything. Just see if you're really interested in what I am saying.

I will never get it, I believe.

In the end, it's not important if you "get it" or not. What you believe you are, a seeker, will never get it. What you really are – pure awareness – is already it. In other words, you are already That.

I can't believe that.

I know. You are still thinking as a person. It's *what you really are* I am referring to. Not the person.

What I really am is already it?

Sure. No less than me or anyone else.

9

Two sides
of the same coin

*In contrast to some spiritual schools, this philosophy of
yours is not dogmatic. Although I don't like everything
you say, I can't think of any way to criticise what you
write in your books.*

Still most people seem to believe the religious stories.

*How come so many people – even quite intelligent people
– are willing to believe all the religious stories? How come
that they are willing to accept the authority of a so-called
holy book?*

I don't know. Maybe people are afraid of death. Maybe
they look for certainty in this world. Apparently it's
part of some mass hypnosis. It seems to be attractive
because it's always been very popular to believe in
higher forces.

*Even before there was any organized religion, humans did
rituals to influence the natural elements or to celebrate*

the first rain. Or to honour the sun or the moon. Animals never have ceremonies, I believe.

It seems to be a typical characteristic of humanity. I don't want to stop this, some ceremonies are very beautiful.

Some religions seem to help certain people at some level.

Sure. It seems to give some people hope or a sense of security. Especially in times of war or conflict.

Right. It seems to help people temporarily. And you don't want to take that away from those people who "need" such a religion.

I just point to the fact that a lot of things we believe are rather a matter of belief.

What you say demands no belief whatsoever.

It's more a matter of *seeing* than believing – although there is nobody who can "see" it.

Why do most people not understand what you say?

It's impossible to understand it. The mind can't get this.

That's why it's unattractive for the mind. Unattractive for the ego.

This vision leaves the seeker with nothing to do. With nobody to judge.

That's another problem. Most people love to judge others. You take away that possibility.

The ego doesn't want to be destroyed. But on the other hand I have to add here that the ego can't be destroyed or doesn't have to be destroyed because there is no ego in the first place.

Most people can't see the simplicity of all this. Or they simply don't want to see it. Can't you change others so they see this as well?

I don't want to change people. That would be contradictory to everything I said earlier. Why would I try to destroy these belief systems? Why would I try to liberate other egos if there is nobody there?

They can't help it anyway if they "see" this or not, can they?

If there is no person, there is no free will.

So they can't help it. I can't blame anyone.

Right. Nobody to blame, nobody to criticize. How about that?

10 |

There is always
a shadow side

*You say in your book that there is no right without left
and that fighting the left is useless.*

I can't stop people from judging each other. I can't stop
people who believe they are on the right side from
fighting those on the left side. All I do is point to the
conceptual nature of the line between left and right.

*But people don't like what you say because then they can't
fight against the left guys any more. The Americans can't
fight the terrorists any more and the Muslims can't criticize the Americans or the Jews any more. So don't expect
everybody will follow your ideas.*

Black and white are two sides of the same coin. The
Light doesn't notice any demarcation lines. Oneness
doesn't judge. The light source of the movie won't say
that the left side of the screen is the bad side and
the right side of the screen is the good side. From
the point of view of the source of light, there is no
demarcation line.

You say there is no black without a white. Does that mean if we only show our "good" side, we develop at the same time a shadow side which is hidden? I mean, do we develop a beautiful house with a nice "façade" where all the garbage is stored in the cellars?

I am not sure if there is a rule about that. All I can say is that I believe there is always a shadow side. That's a crucial element of the black and white balance. You can't have the sunny side without the shadow side. But it's not always apparent at first sight.

I am Catholic and recently I was shocked by the news about the scandal that originated in Boston, where Catholic priests were abusing boys. I saw a TV programme on this subject. While the Vatican in Rome knew about it, they failed to deal with the problem and just put the priest in another village or town, where that particular priest could continue to abuse young boys. While Rome never offered support or psychological help to the victims, all they did was protect their power. Later investigations showed that this was not just one priest, but that it was endemic. I was shocked. I decided to stop my faith in the Catholic church. They don't practise themselves what they teach to others.

Could be so. They are just taking care of their power. They want to survive. That's what organisations usually do. But it is not up to us to judge these priests or the organisation. That's food for the judges and lawyers of the countries where it happened.

You don't care?

"Seeing" that everything is always in balance, doesn't mean that the actor called "Jan" has to approve what happened. Or that Jan has to like it. Or leave it unpunished.

What could be your reaction then? Amazed? Surprised? Sad?

As a person, I can say that I would feel sorry for the victims and their parents if all the accusations turned out to be true. As a medical doctor I might think about the psychological damage, for example. My human reaction – as an actor in the appearance - would probably be something like that. So, in the appearance others would say about me that "I" am caring about the victims. But other actors maybe react in another way.

Yes, you're right. Some people might say that these priests should be put in prison immediately. Or executed. A psychiatrist might say that these priests were abused themselves by their own uncles or teachers, and that they couldn't control their behaviour. The Catholic leaders in Rome might deny the facts, or try and sweep the problem under the carpet. Some of the parents of these boys might even go to a shop and buy a gun to kill these same priests to prevent them from doing it again.

Who knows what other comments or reactions might arise?

But don't you see there are all sorts of problems that have to be taken care of? I mean, if you say that everything is as it is, then it sounds as if you don't care about anything any more.

I know it sometimes looks that way. But let me tell you it's rather the opposite. I've been told this before. Realising that everything is Oneness is not the same as indifference.

Still, the abuse of the young boys is a sad story, isn't it?

Yes, of course.

Is what happened yet another example of the shadow side? Of the law of the black and white balance you talk about in your books?

Yes, could be. Although I am not sure if it is really a law, like for example the law of gravity. But I agree that everything has its shadow side. No north pole without a south pole.

I believe that a church which denies natural forces – such as sexuality - and suppresses these forces by requiring celibacy of their priests, will sooner or later be confronted with the dark cellars of these dogmas. I mean, they will be faced with the shadow sides. Don't think it is just happening with Catholic priests. Every religion has similar stories – although the majority of them are kept quiet.

Your story of the abuse of young boys by these priests

may indeed illustrate that if you suppress something natural, it will come out via some sort of subway. Some underground phenomenon that will surface one day or another.

One can't suppress sexual forces. Whether you are a priest or a monk or whatever. It will come out anyway.

A similar story is told in the movie *Samsara*. This movie is the story of the spiritual quest of a monk, filmed in Ladakh. Tashi, who has been a monk since age five, finds himself challenged by women.

By suppressed sexual energies.

Right. He leaves the monastery and finds out about the outside world, about *samsara*.

I loved that movie. The landscapes, the music.

The director has a critical approach to life in a monastery, and to the patriarchal approach of spiritual traditions. It's also interesting to see how his wife Pema has more wisdom about the essence of Buddhism and that she dares to criticise Buddha's decision to leave his wife and son in the middle of the night.

Anyway, the movie showed that even Buddhist monks have to deal with a shadow side. One can't suppress natural forces.

Whether you are a priest or a monk. Or whatever you

do in life. There is always a shadow side to everyone and everything.

But still it's obvious that both the bright side as well as the dark side are two sides of the same coin. Both are equal expressions of Oneness.

Both are always in balance. The black side can't cover or hide the white side. One is not bigger than the other one. Or better.

Oneness always has both sides. And they are in balance – despite the appearances of imbalance.

11 |

It feels as if
I can choose

Is there nothing we can do to change the world for the better?

Why would you do that?

I see a lot of suffering.

There is also a lot of love in the world.

I want to help those who suffer.

Some seem to take care of others, while other people seem to start wars and terror.

And those who start the war also believe that they are doing the right thing! If you would have asked Bush or Blair about the war in Iraq, they would answer that they were absolutely sure that they did the right thing.

Do you believe they have a choice?

If they have no ego, than they have no volition. So I can't blame them. That's very hard to accept. I prefer to make them responsible for all those innocent people killed during the war in Iraq.

I understand. But if there is no person, there is no choice.

Well, I don't agree with what both of you are saying there. You can say whatever you like. I know that I have responsibilities. It feels as if I can choose. I want to work on a better world.

If that's what "your actor" is doing on the screen, then that's what's happening. I am not trying to stop you.

Or is it useless because the "bright" I want to create with my good deeds will be compensated by the "dark" side by other deeds? No matter if the dark deeds are done by me or by someone else?

That's what I mean by the law of black and white. But I can't prove it.

Still I feel as if I can choose to help people or not.

Are you sure you can choose?

I think so.

Indeed, you *think* so! Don't you see that it's just another idea?

Another concept?

Right. Another concept, another idea. The idea of having chosen. The idea of there being a decider in your mind.

But still I have chosen a lot of things in my life.

Where is the chooser? Where is the decider?

Well, let me say that certain decisions have arisen in my mind.

If you watch your mind, you will see that thoughts arise of their own accord. When you investigate what appears, it becomes clear that you are not the thinker of your thoughts; thoughts just appear and disappear in your movie. Well, in what appears to be your movie, because the latter is just another thought.

But I can choose my thoughts, can't I? About an hour ago the lady asked me if I wanted coffee or tea. I took a cup of tea. So I chose tea! Listen to what I say, I chose tea! Don't come and tell me that I can't choose. You're choosing yourself all the time. You asked for sparkling water. You can't fool me with all your cheap tricks.

What if that idea of choice is just another snap shot, appearing as one of the thousands of images that appear in a day?

You will have to show me.

Let's say that about ten thousand images appear in "your" mind every day. Impressions of warm and cold, sadness or thirst, visual images, hopes and fears, lust and hunger, insights, tactile sensations, and so on. If we accept the linear time axis, it looks like a long train of images.

OK.

When this lady asked if you wanted coffee or tea, this is a scenario of what may happen during the next seconds. Thought no. 2,233 says "This coffee has a great smell." Thought no. 2,234 says "I am going to drink coffee" and thought no. 2,235 says, "Maybe I will not sleep well tonight after coffee" and then thought no. 2,236 says, "Green tea is better for my health" and then you say, "Tea, please." That's 2,237. Then your hand goes to pick up a tea bag. That's 2,238. Then you say to yourself that you have decided to drink tea. The latter is image no. 2,239. And then you drink tea and sense its taste. That is image no. 2,240.

OK.

In reality, many more images pass by, of course. And they do so at a much faster speed. A faster speed than I can ever tell you. But the question is, do you believe that image no. 2,238 causes image no. 2,239?

It's all just a movie then, and nobody is in control? Is it all programmed then?

No, it's not programmed. The idea of a programmer or a director would be thought no. 2,245! Images just appear and disappear.

I see. They come and go all the time. Like a train that passes along.

Images that continuously appear on "your" plasma screen can be images about warm or cold, heaven or hell, tea or coffee, yesterday or tomorrow, and so on. But the point here is whether one image *causes* the next image.

It looks that way. But you're going to say that that's just image no. 2,239.

The question is, have you really chosen to drink tea, or was it just another snapshot? As all "your" apparent decisions and choices are also thoughts appearing and disappearing, you can ask yourself whether you really decide or whether apparent decisions just appear. To act upon a certain thought feels like choice – afterwards – and is labelled as free will or choice by the ego. The ego uses language for that. But it's hard to prove you have chosen.

So you're just a robot without free will?

There is actually no individual here to have its own free will or to be deprived of free will. The thought of "me" and the thoughts of tea or coffee merely unfold as a manifestation of Beingness. They are all expressions of the energy of Beingness, if you like such a description. They are all apparent reflections of Pure Awareness.

From your perspective, there is a sense that life is simply happening?

There is a sense that life is simply happening, yes. But it is not *me* who is witnessing life. Then my ego would put itself back in the central position. It's not "my" life. It's just life.

I see. You're the witness.

Don't try to personalise the witness.

OK. You're the impersonal witness then.

Saying "impersonal" is not the same as impersonal.

Is that another trick of the Advaita *school? To say it's an impersonal liberation, while at the same time they're still telling you what to do?*

Right.

It's incredible. To talk about an impersonal liberation, and then telling people how to save the world?

Yes!

I read it somewhere in the What is Enlightenment *journal.*

The author of that article was talking about Advaita *and in the same journal he asked if enlightenment can save the world! Isn't it ridiculous?*

It may reflect a lack of clarity at that point. But even such lack of clarity is OK.

It's the same with the authors who say that in 2,012 the world will go into a new era. Or we will fail and will head for a disaster, or we prevail and go to a higher dimension. It's like the Jehovah's who predicted that the world would disappear on a particular day. But that was maybe three decades ago!

I know.

People just love stories about conspiracies or about secret clubs. Or about disasters coming up.

Yes. Such theories are quite popular. But they mean absolutely nothing to Beingness.

12

I want to stay in control

You said the "me" is just an idea. I am willing to accept that for a moment. If there is no separate "me," there can't be even the question of there being free will, can there? If there is no linear time axis, there can't be a question about destination, can there? It's all in the mind then?

Things are just happening. And they're not happening *to me*, they just *appear* to be happening to me. And they're not happening to you either, they just *appear* to be happening to you.

So you just sit on your sofa and wait for something to happen?

This understanding does not necessarily mean doing nothing in the sense of laziness, but rather that everything is happening spontaneously and of its own accord.

It sounds like doing nothing at all.

The Taoists call this "Wu Wei", which translates as non-doing while things are still happening.

Everything happens without a plan? Just effortlessly?

Less is done, while nothing is left undone.

Still, the idea of our actions happening by themselves instead of through our free will can be confusing. As a Christian, I regard free will as an inherent quality of my personal individuality. I also see it as a gift from God to see if I am strong enough to resist evil forces. So what you say is totally unacceptable to me. I need to do the right thing.

From the personal point of view, the idea that Beingness is living through us can be quite threatening. It seems to reduce us to mere robots, implying a lack of creativity and self-awareness. It also implies a sort of helplessness and even the sense of being stupid or lazy. Or that we have a lack of personality.

If actions are not our own actions, then we can do whatever we want?

Are you looking for an excuse for undesirable behaviour?

No, it's just the opposite. I want to be aware of ethics, morality and be a good human being. Your theory is undermining that.

What is overlooked in such arguments is that *all activity*

is of Beingness, appearing as the multiplicity of characters that apparently do the acting and choosing.

Both the moral deeds as well as the immoral deeds are expressions of Oneness? Both the ego of the murderer as well as the ego of the victim are images on a screen? They're both concepts or appearances? And nobody decides or controls anything?

Doesn't sound nice, but check it out for yourself. Don't believe it because I said so.

OK. But my ego is not going to like this.

But "your" ego is but a phantom. And that phantom wants to stay in control.

The ego still wants to be the captain?

The person wants to survive. That's how it's designed.

The ego claims it is the decider?

Right. And it really feels as if you *really* are real. And that *you* decide.

But now you make me feel useless. Unpredictable. Like a robot.

Your ego doesn't like it that its mechanisms of survival are exposed the way I am unmasking them. So I am not surprised your ego is fighting back.

Right. I feel resistance as you talk. Or should I say, my ego resists your philosophy.

"Your" ego doesn't like my words.

I want to stay in control, whatever it costs.

It's like the child who doesn't want to let go of the steering wheel of one of these big toy cars at the entrance of the shopping mall. Although the car doesn't move, the child enjoys the ride. It pretends to have control although the child knows there is no control at all.

We want to believe we are in control.

We hold onto our belief in free choice.

We resist the idea of being helpless. The ego hates to be helpless. The person wants to hold the steering wheel. The ego believes that past and future are for real.

That's how the movie is designed.

But even when we can't choose, we are still the doer of our deeds, aren't we? Or is that also another concept?

The ego is neither the doer nor the non-doer. And why is that? Because the idea of being the doer is just another concept. Can a concept create the next deed? Can a thought create the next action? You assume that

71

to be true, but is that so? Some thoughts are acted upon, and others are not. There are no rules.

What about my personality then?

The ego simply hasn't an existence independent of Beingness.

What happened to your ego then?

Don't assume that "my ego" was there in the first place.

It was in my mind. Because I was thinking about you. I had an image of you in my mind.

Right.

Still let's assume there is an ego – in the appearance.

The ego is something which has never been there – except as an idea. Whether that is in my brain or in yours, it doesn't matter. There simply is no one sitting here.

Well, I assume there is a person sitting in front of me. What about that man called "Jan"? What can your books teach me about you?

First let me tell you that my books are not about me, but about "That" which doesn't exclude you or me or anyone else.

OK. Still, there seems to be a difference between you and

me. I still feel as if I am identifying with my ego and my personal story.

What happens is more like a falling away of the belief in the importance of the ego. The sense of a personal self is a mixture of concepts. It's made of a system of ideas, memories, emotions and a lot of conditioning. This mental structure has been built up over the years and appears to be very solid. And yet, it's nothing but a concept. An idea.

So you believe you don't have an ego?

No. Not at all. Who would say that there is no ego? Can Jan number one talk to Jan number two and say that number two does not exist?

It's silly.

Can the "me" deny the "me"? Thinking "I have an ego" is just a thought, and so is thinking "I don't have an ego." Both are concepts which include "me" along with "ego", and both appear and disappear on the plasma screen. They don't appear to Jan.

So the images and ideas I have about myself don't prove that my personality really exists?

That's right.

13

When will
I understand this?

When will I understand what you seem to have under-stood?

It's not "you" who will understand. There is no "you" and there is no future moment.

I don't follow.

There is no future moment where the ego will disappear. The ego never existed anyway. How can you expect the nonexistent to disappear?

Sometimes people have had special experiences where everything seemed to become clear.

You don't have to wait for a special experience. You don't have to wait for the ego to suddenly disappear. How could it matter when that person who wants such an experience isn't real in the first place?

But such experiences can be very dramatic.

And even if you believe you have had a major transcendental event, what does it matter? Maybe it's no more than a few brain waves that change. Professor Newberg used a special scanner to visualise very subtle brain changes in real time. He examined nuns and monks and explained their transcendental phenomena as a brain thing – like one can have with LSD.

People won't like to hear their transcendental events being reduced by a scientist to brain chemicals or brain currents.

Right. But these scientists like Newberg could be right.

I don't have to wait for grace to take away the sense of self.

Beingness already sees and contains the hearing of these words and the arising of thoughts, which then are identified as "your" thoughts. What "you" really are is Beingness and the totality of its content – although it looks as though you're only a human locked up in a body.

So you suggest that there is Beingness on the one hand and its content on the other?

No. That's why I use the metaphor of the plasma screen. It's the screen on which your movie appears. The white screen, the light source and the images that appear on the movie screen can't be separated one from the other. It's a nice metaphor, but they are not three different things. In truth, there is nothing but Beingness. There is no ego to either understand it or not understand it. There is only Beingness.

When the ego is unmasked, do you feel lighter?

Your question is about the person. What does it matter if the person believes he or she is lighter after the understanding once it's clear that there is no one?

Are you happier then before?

Your question is again about me. About the person. Your ego hopes – by understanding this philosophy – to become happier or to have less problems. Some teachers of *Advaita* say that the majority of your problems will melt away when the ego is unmasked. When they say that, they are talking to the reader. They're talking to *"you"*! While ten minutes earlier they said there is no "you".

I see. It's contradictory. You're right.

Most books on spirituality are about the seeker. About *you* improving. In the future. My books make it clear that there is no "you" so don't expect any homework from me!

I see. It reminds me of the three major belief systems you mentioned in This Is It.

It's again about the person, about the future, about

improvement. These are the three major cards the ego uses to continue its play. To continue to be at the centre. The ego has all sorts of cards to continue playing its role.

While all I have to do is see that there is no one.

Well, you don't have to *do* anything. Who would be doing it? Where is the "you" who is planning to see that there is no one? It's a paradox. It's like a Zen koan.

Right.

If I suggested that things will go better after the understanding, I would be talking to you as a person. Wouldn't that be contradictory when five minutes ago I tried to explain that this person – mine as well as yours – is only a ghost?

But life goes on, doesn't it?

The ego you thought you were continues to play its role as a dreamed character.

Right.

It's just one of the many guises of Beingness. But as it is clear that the real "you" is much bigger, there is no longer any effort dedicated to worrying about all the theories and concepts you believed in before.

14 |

Pointing at the sun

You suggest that as long as there is a need for religious symbols, spiritual practices or taking seriously all these personal spiritual stories, there is still no complete understanding of the nature of Oneness.

How can there be any need for all that when it's clear that there *is* only Oneness?

There is only Oneness?

And there is only one of it. There is nothing else. So why change this Oneness? You can't step out of it.

I see.

Why create a rigid belief system with heaven and hell? Why pray three times a day? Why go on a pilgrimage? Why create spiritual heroes if this Oneness knows no hierarchies?

Well, it may help people who are looking for a path. A

path to find their true self.

The idea of separation is only a concept, and so are all the religious rules and paths.

But people want answers to their questions.

Religions don't want to answer the *real* questions. All they do is come up with stories, rules and hierarchies. They avoid what I am saying in my books at any cost.

Aren't there any exceptions?

Yes. At the core of each religion is a wisdom that comes close to this. But words will fail anyway.

Are we closer to this understanding as young children?

As a newborn, there is no sense of separation. A baby doesn't know there is a "me" and a "not-me". When you grow up, your sense of Oneness moves into the background as you identify yourself with the person, with the body. As soon as there is the belief in a "me," there must be "other than me".

You draw a line. A line between "me" and "not-me". A line between past and future. That is where dualism starts. That's when the trouble begins.

The human mind has the habit of dividing the content of consciousness into two parts: part one, called "me", and part two called "not-me." This part one / part two division is practical for our vision of the world, for our sense of being a human being.

Part one is the "me" living in this body and part two refers to "the rest of the world".

I am "here" and not-me is over there.

The mind draws a line.

An imaginary line. Such a division is conceptual.

And you say that this division is essential for everyday life but that it is counterproductive when we are looking for the essence of what we are.

Well, it's just a belief system.

After the understanding that there is only Oneness, the whole division into "me" and "the rest of the world" is put in perspective. At first sight, your books turn our whole view of the world upside down.

It's hard to believe that there is only Oneness. And it's even harder to believe that what you really are is that same Oneness.

It doesn't seem to make sense.

It is not meant to make sense. If there is only Being-ness in which *all* happenings take place, then this division into part one and two are just concepts in our minds. In fact, even the demarcation line between the two parts occurs in the same awareness. So even the false sense of separation is equally Beingness. That's why one can say that Beingness has always been the case, before as well as after the understanding. There isn't even a before or after. All these demarcation lines seem to melt away when there is true understanding about the nature of Beingness.

What's the trouble with the separation between "me" and "the rest of the world"?

There is nothing wrong with it. It's even very practical in everyday life. In the daydream. In the novel. All I say is that "you" are so much more than that body-mind.

With that idea of separation, a certain sense of fragility appears here. What about pain and disease? What happens when I die? Will I go to hell because I've been a bad boy?

All that can make you afraid, vulnerable. So many unanswered questions. Most religions take advantage of that. They pretend to know the answers. But they don't know the answers at all. They all say different things! They all have different scenarios, different dogmas.

They don't know. They just pretend to know. Or they believe their own beliefs.

First they will confirm that you are a person. They will not show you the texts that tell you that you are not the person.

And then they say I am a person with a past and a future. Maybe also a soul. Or with a higher task.

And then they will also tell you what to do. Or what to avoid.

And you don't need any religion anymore?

You don't need any religion to recognize that we are all one, do you? To see that we are all equal expressions of Oneness? It's rather the opposite: the religions point to hierarchies, dogmas and heroes, not to Oneness. I try to point at that which is accessible for all of us. And the paradox is that nobody gets it. Nobody can get this as a person.

Are you like the Zen masters, who say that the finger pointing to the moon is not the moon?

I would rather say I try to point at the sun instead of the moon. And the sun stands here for the one and only source of light of everything. Of all beings.

15 |

Democratic spirituality

The way you talk about Beingness doesn't sound very exclusive. Your vision is very democratic. Before I read your book Coming Home *I believed that seeing the ultimate truth was exclusive for the special ones. For the gurus, saints and seers.*

That's another story to make the seeker continue to stay on the path.

So, anyone can see this?

The Beingness I refer to is something we all *are*. No exception. Nobody is excluded. Everyone is it.

Can any seeker see this without the help of a guru or spiritual teaching?

Every seeker *is* it. It's not something you can see.

But not all spiritual teachers say so.

Some teachers may point you to Oneness and others may point you to duality. Some will give you hope and some will unmask your expectations. It depends on what kind of teacher you're attracted to. But Oneness can't be learned. You don't need holy books to see that *everything* is holy. You don't need any special event – for example, an awakening experience or some spectacular epiphany - to prove to yourself that your true nature is Beingness. You are already That. This Beingness is not dependent on the absence or the presence of the actor. If the ego appears – apparently – that's just another image on the screen. If it appears, it's just an image appearing for a split second. If you think you're in an egoless state, then that's another image on the plasma screen. As soon as there is an understanding that there is nothing to find, that there is nothing to achieve, then it's obvious that there are no spiritual rules to follow.

No rules at all?

The spiritual leaders of the formal religions won't like it, of course. Most of them want to keep their clothes, their holy places, their symbols, their power, their dogmas, their holy books.

So, if I understand what you're saying, all spiritual theories are just ideas, theories of the human mind.

Yes, most of them are games of the human mind. Well, not all of them are pointing to dualism, of course. Some texts try indeed to point to Oneness instead of pointing to hierarchies. If you look carefully, you can find them in any tradition. But they're not so popular.

It's in the core of each religion.

Yes. If you look carefully, you can recognize it in the core of each religion or spiritual tradition. However, all that books can offer are concepts. They may serve as pointers to That which can't be reached by words or theories. But they can easily be misunderstood.

So I can't take your words as the truth because your words are dualistic as well.

Yes, indeed. The words in my books are not written in stone. If you take them for the absolute truth, you are back into a belief system. Very soon, they would become new dogmas. So everything I say is just a limited way of trying to point to what is limitless. Even this interview set-up is dualistic because it presupposes a first character (you) who doesn't know and another character (Jan) who does know. That's maybe true if you ask me questions about medical techniques like Biopuncture, but not relevant when talking about Beingness. We can't talk about what we are, we can only discuss different concepts. About different angles to approach the unapproachable.

And this boundless energy is what we are? Even when I feel I am in conflict with the world?

Nothing can cover this boundless Energy. You are that

which is prior to any kind of peace or conflict, prior to every thought or feeling.

I don't feel that way.

You don't have to. I've said it before, you don't have to see it or feel it. That's impossible because it's what you are. You can't feel the light because you are the light.

I see.

You may believe "you" have all sorts of special experiences that prove you're coming closer to "it". But that's another game.

That's another story.

All these perceptions are concepts appearing and disappearing within the Light that you are. You don't need the fulfilment of any kind of seeking in order to be what you already are. You don't need a spiritual technique to see that you are already Beingness.

Even when I feel frustrated or when I am in pain?

Sure. Even when you feel limited to that body. Even when you identify with your ego. Remember, nothing is excluded. You are a perfect expression of this single boundless energy. And that boundlessness is what *you* are.

If a seeker has excellent understanding of what you say,

*really knows without doubt that there is nobody there,
does it really matter that there is still a subtle sense of
identity there?*

No, it doesn't matter. As I said earlier, that subtle sense
would be just a snapshot. Nothing more. How could it
possibly matter? And again, *to whom* could it matter?
To the phantom that is clearly seen as a phantom?

I see.

Trying to finally dispose of the ego might appear to
be another task. And whose task is it? Again, a task
for the ego. The seeker asking himself if he or she
is doing all right? Wondering if one has to wait until
the opening of the heart? The ego tries another game,
continuously wondering if it's doing OK. "If I do or
feel like that, am I already enlightened or not?" or, "I
just was angry at my partner, so I'm still identified
with my emotions, I must not be fully awake yet."
The ego has so many tricks to get itself going. If you
look at it, it's ridiculous. So, when there is what you
call "excellent understanding," such questions simply
won't come up any more.

*I was still subtly hoping that a point in "my path"
would come when there would simply be "no one home"
permanently. A blissful moment of awakening, an
epiphany that would open my heart, clean my soul and
would take away all my problems. That there would
be "pure Being" without any sense of ego or any sense
of time. I realize it's indeed ridiculous to expect that.*

Most seekers create problems where there aren't any. You don't have to get rid of the ego permanently because there is no ego and there is no linear time axis. The image is already gone (and has been replaced by another one) before you can even ask me questions about it.

16 |

Give me hope

I *was told that my soul has chosen this body to learn certain lessons on earth.*

Why is that?

I don't know. My soul has chosen this body to learn certain lessons in the material world so I can evolve to a higher level.

What exactly is this soul you talk about? Maybe it's just a concept in your brain? What if "your" soul is just another concept appearing in your mind as a few chemicals?

To me, the soul is more than just a few electrical currents in my brain. It's my higher self. And even if it was a concept in my mind, what's wrong with it? I mean, my mission on this planet is important, and one has to discover why one is here on earth. We have to work on the planet's evolution.

How can there be an evolution if the future is a mind construct?

We have to work on the planet's evolution. We also have to work on our own evolution.

That's what you say.

And moreover, when you die, your soul goes to heaven or to hell according to the way you have lived. So you had better watch out with what you say.

Some believe seventy-seven virgins are waiting for them if they walk into a subway with a bomb in their back pack. In the last 5,000 years, so many stories have been told. For example, the Pharaohs of Egypt believed they needed a boat to cross the river to the after-life.

OK. That's not something I would believe in. But there are other things I believe in. I am a spiritual seeker. And I am looking for a higher level of consciousness.

How can you look for a higher level if you're already every level? When "you" are already all and everything? If your "me" is an illusion, all your plans and questions about that "me" melt away.

I don't agree. You seem to say that everything is an illusion.

The illusion looks so real that we take it for real.

90

My senses and my programming keep shouting at me that I am a person in this body. I can't help it. The only way out so far for me was identifying myself with the witness. That brought me a sort of peace. Say a temporary calmness in my mind. I thought I was coming closer to liberation that way. But you took away all my dreams about getting full awakening.

That's just a game of the ego. We like to believe there is both a witness and that which is witnessed. But that's dualistic again. So the ego might claim the role of "witnesser" and look at the world from a distance. The "witnesser" *here* and the rest of the world "over there." That may indeed feel peaceful sometimes. And that makes it attractive for the seeker. The ego loves spiritual goals. The personality also likes problems which confirm its existence.

Like?

For example, that it is difficult to find your true nature. That you have to go through the dark night of the soul. It is just a way to keep going. To give yourself hope. To confirm that you're on a path to salvation.

The ego wants a path to follow.

Right. While there is nowhere to go.

I always believed I could make progress on the spiritual path by following the rules of my spiritual community. Until I started to read your books.

You believed "you" were coming closer. But that's another illusion, another thought. The screen and the watcher and the source of light are not separate as in a real movie theatre, they are one and undivided. It's the plasma screen I told you about before. You can't come closer to what you really are!

I would prefer you to give me hope again.

If I were to give you hope, I would be talking *to the person*. There are thousands of books that will give you hope. They promise you that in seven steps you will find peace of mind or fulfil all your dreams. They propose that you ask yourself why you are here. They will ask you what your goals are. They will tell you what your soul can learn in this lifetime. They will tell you what you can do to make more right in this world and less left. If that's what you look for here, you will be disappointed.

I am.

Your ego will probably say that you're sitting in the wrong class here because it can't play its games. The ego wants to run away from this.

I see. But I hoped to come closer to my true nature. That I would learn to deal with my emotions. Especially the dark ones.

Notice that the witness of the thoughts and the thoughts themselves are made of the same substance. Both the idea of "you" as well as the nice thoughts *and* the dark thoughts are made of the same substance. They *are* one thing. Notice that the witness of "your" emotions and the emotions themselves are made of the same light. They are all waves in one big endless ocean.

They're made of the same substance?

It's as simple as that! The perceiver of an emotion – the person you believe yourself to be – and the emotion itself are both electrical currents in the brain. Both are images on the screen.

I don't understand.

Even on a biochemical level there is already Oneness. Both the person you believe you are as well as your physical sensations and your thoughts are made of the same molecules – say, hydrogen, oxygen, sodium, potassium, carbon and a few others.

That's the story of the sandcastle and the sand grains again. But what about the world around me?

Even on a bioelectrical level, all emotions and beliefs are made of the same substance, some electrons moving around and creating thoughts and emotions in your brain. And these same electrons also build up the world which you say is around you.

But still I believe that ...

Watch carefully what you're saying here. You said, "believe". It's another belief, whatever you were going to say.

It would be better if I remained silent. All these thoughts and comments only make things worse.

You don't have to try and suppress what's appearing. The comments are images as well. They have less meaning than most people believe. Language is a system of the human brain to give meaning to the sensations that occur. But it is all metaphorical.

The world outside is a construction of the brain then? Well, that's what some people say. It's the human brain that creates all I see and feel. Some say I even create who I will meet in life. It's all in my mind.

But what these guys usually forget to say is that the brain which is supposed to do all this creating is itself also part of the illusion!

So that theory is just an intermediate step.

I would add that the brain and the person who says all this are also – I know I am always saying the same thing - images on the screen.

17

All is an illusion

If nothing is to be attained here, why do so many books say I can do this or should avoid that?

Seekers want something to do. The ego needs a tool or a goal in order to survive. So they create a story. They create a system with rules.

They also say that everything is an illusion. Still the world around me feels very solid.

Quantum physics says that more than 99.99% of solid matter is empty space.

I know. But still I see you sitting on a chair.

Neuroscience says that when you see something, there is a delay. It takes a while before the light reaches your eyes. If you see a star, the star could already be "dead" by the time the light reaches the earth. The same goes for sound, because that's even slower.

What about touch?

Same thing. It takes some time before the sensation in your toe reaches your brain.

And a lot of sensations are filtered as well. We have an input of millions of impressions and data, while the brain filters them in order to focus on just a few little items. Otherwise we wouldn't survive.

But there is something else. What you believe you decided has also already happened before you can tell me or anyone else.

How do you mean?

For example, you scratch your cheek. It has already happened before you notice. First the brain waves or the brain chemicals change, and then the arm and the hand start to move.

OK. But that's not a good example. Say I want to raise my hand. I did it right now. You see, I have just proved that you are wrong. I just decided to raise my hand!

Neuroscientists like Professor Libet in the USA will say that the current in your brain that causes you to raise your hand already happened a few milliseconds before it happened.

OK. But even then, I can say that I have taken the decision in my own brain?

Maybe you haven't been to one of these meetings before, otherwise you would know what I am going to say to that remark.

What is that?

Try to find that person who took the decision. If you can't find it now, take your time and do it at home. Or go and see a radiologist who will take a brain scan. Or just close your eyes and go searching for this person in your head, or if you prefer this feeling in your chest or belly. When you have found your "I" please let me know.

Well ...

You can email me, fax me, call me or whatever. I have asked this many times before, and so far, nobody has ever come up with an answer.

Other books by Jan Kersschot

Coming Home (Inspiration 2001, Editions India 2007)

Nobody Home (Watkins 2003, New Age Books India 2005)
Also in Dutch, German, Spanish, Russian

This Is It (Watkins 2004)
Also in Dutch and Korean

Beingness (Editions India 2007) Will also appear in Dutch and French

Biopuncture and Antihomotoxic Medicine (Inspiration 1998) Also in Spanish, Russian

Biopuncture in General Practice (Inspiration 2004)

For further information and a current list of books in print, please visit: www.kersschot.com

Other Titles from Non-Duality Press

Lightning Source UK Ltd.
Milton Keynes UK
UKOW041406020513

210106UK00001B/27/A

9 780955 399961